IMAGES
OF
ISRAEL

D0756481

PHOTOGRAPHY BY
HANAN ISACHAR

APOGEE
PRESS

Photographs copyright © 1994 Hanan Isachar
Text copyright © 1994 with the publisher
Published by Apogee Press
P.O. Box 5634, Herzlia 46150, Israel.
All rights reserved.

Introduction by Danny Ben-Tal
and Hedva Isachar Canetti
Captions by Hedva Isachar Canetti
Translated by Leeanne Shilo
Designed by Roni Kourtz

Printed in Singapore.

ISBN 965-222-463-4

IMAGES
OF
ISRAEL

Above: Moonrise over the wall of old Jerusalem.

Front cover: Mount Arbel, overlooking the Sea of Galilee (Kinneret), in the waning light.

Title spread: The western section of the wall of the Old City of Jerusalem. It was built by the Ottoman sultan, Suleiman the Magnificent, between 1535 - 1538. The stones in the lower half of the wall are from the crusader period. The minaret which dominates the southern portion of the citadel was built by the Ottomans.

Pages 4-5: A serene view of the Sea of Galilee.

Pages 6-7: Curious glances, glistening in anticipation of the wedding of the son of the Belzer rebbe in the Belz Hassidic community in Jerusalem.

Pages 8-9: An olive grove in Ein Karem.

IMAGES OF ISRAEL

INTRODUCTION

Every long journey begins with one short step, guides the Chinese proverb. The first-time visitor to Israel might imagine that with one short step he will cross the narrow waist of the country, while two steps would suffice to cover the 555 kilometers which separate Israel's northernmost city, Metulla, from its southernmost, Eilat. The more he or she travels, however, the more the visitor will be delighted by a surprising discovery: the more one learns of Israel's natural landscapes and its rich cultural landscapes, which are a mosaic of customs and traditions of local residents and of a myriad of immigrants, the larger Israel becomes. The ingathering of the Jews of the world to Israel, and indeed the revival of the Hebrew language, are wonders not only to those who observe Israel from outside, but to those who reside in the country as well. The foundations of the Israel of today are laid deep within this land. Their traces are found in thousands of archaeological sites across the land itself, as well as in the history of the land, the peoples whose fate has been linked with it, and its many conquerors throughout the ages.

Bounded by Lebanon in the north, Syria in the northeast, Jordan in the east and Egypt in the southwest, the country encompasses an unparalleled variety of landscapes: from the lowest point on earth, the Dead Sea, which is 398 meters below sea level, to wind-lashed hilltops, lush pasturelands, pine forests, arid deserts, asteroid craters, white sandy beaches, multicolored underwater worlds and cavernous stalactite caves. The state's borders have changed dramatically since the 1948 War of Independence, altering Israel's area, which is officially cited as 20,700 square kilometers. Israel's only certain border is its western border, the Mediterranean Sea, which moderates the region's weather, but also challenges Israelis to define and constantly redefine their relationships with this place and their existence in this crossroads between East and West.

Perhaps the love of Israel's hiking trails which characterizes many Israelis is itself part of the quest for a link with the land, a search for the roots of the new Israeli. The echoes of that divine command which Abraham heard —"Get thee out of thy country and from thy kindred and from thy father's house, to the land that I will show thee"— continue to reverberate throughout the region and produce a variety of tunes, based on the personal views of the interpreter. Hiking is seen as a way of becoming familiar with the land, "conquering" the ground, forging a link with landscapes that preserve the national memory.

Israel's geographic location enables the country to be a loving nursery for plants of northern climates as well as for desert flora. About 2400 different species of wild flowers grow in Israel. Most of the vegetation is defined as Mediterranean, but various tropical species may also be found. The region and its subtropical climate provide a comfortable habitat for animal life and for humans. This fact made possible the development of a rich prehistoric culture unique to this area, as has been revealed by the extensive archaeological excavations that have been conducted throughout the land of Israel.

The cumulative knowledge gathered from modern research is supplemented by the book of Genesis, which teaches us details of the time of the forefathers of the Hebrew nation, beginning with Abraham.

In the first half of the second millenium B.C. Abraham left Ur-Casdim, which lies within modern Iraq, and arrived in Canaan. He traveled the land, wandering with his herds and seeking grazing lands. His son Isaac abandoned nomadism as a way of life, settled upon and worked the land. Jacob, Abraham's grandson, together with his own sons, emigrated to

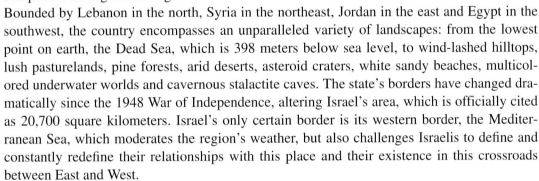

Egypt during a period of severe drought.

Only in the 13th century B.C. did Joshua, heir to Moses, return to Canaan. He led the tribes of Israel, conquered extensive areas of the land and divided it among the tribes.

The period of the kings Saul and David was an era of building and economic growth. David established his capital in the Jebusite city of Jerusalem around 1000 B.C., and Solomon built the Temple there, turning Israel and Jerusalem, capital of the united kingdom, into an international cultural center. Following Solomon's death, the kingdom was divided (in the mid-10th century B.C.) into Israel and Judea, two small and quarreling kingdoms.

In the 8th century B.C. the Assyrians demolished the kingdom of Israel, and in 586 B.C. Nebuchadnezzar, the Babylonian king, conquered Judea, burned the Temple, and expelled most of the Jews into exile in Babylonia.

About sixty years later Cyrus founded the Persian Empire, which was the largest in the ancient East, and he made his famous declaration regarding the right of the Jews to return to Zion and Jerusalem.

The Persian era was brought to an end in Judea by Alexander the Great, who began the Hellenistic Period in the land of Israel in the 4th century B.C. This period saw religious wars between the supporters of the Hellenic culture and the Jewish zealots, culminating in the Hasmonean revolt (164 B.C.) and the redemption of Jerusalem by Judah Maccabee.

The civil wars in Judea continued during the period of the Hasmonean dynasty, the actions of whose sons and daughters brought about the fall of Judea and the conquest of Jerusalem by the armies of the Roman general Pompeius, who destroyed the ruling Hasmonean dynasty (63 B.C.).

The period during which Herod ruled in Judea under the auspices of the Romans (37-4 B.C.) was characterized by the persecution of the remainder of the Hasmonean dynasty and the cruel suppression of its supporters, but was also typified by massive building in Caesarea, Masada, Jericho and especially in Jerusalem, where the Temple was built anew.

During this period Jesus of Nazareth gathered his believers around him. He prayed and preached in the Galilee (27 A.D.), and was tried and crucified in Jerusalem three years later, as related in the New Testament.

From the razing of the Second Temple by Titus in 70 A.D. until the division of the Roman Empire in the middle of the 5th century A.D., Judea was an independent province under the control of the Roman Legion.

The destruction of the Temple and the subsequent dispersion of the Jews in the world necessitated answers to questions relevant to the observance of religious commandments and Jewish practices. To this end, the sages of Israel developed religious and legal institutions and gathered the wisdom of Jewish law passed down from the previous generations. The shaping of the Mishna—which is the Oral Bible and its commentary, the Talmud— was not ceased even after the revolt by Bar Kochba against the Roman emperor Hadrianus and its suppression (135 A.D.), and the founding of Aelia Capitolina, the pagan city in the razed Jerusalem which Jews were not permitted to enter.

The Jews maintained a continuity in the land of Israel during the period of the Byzantine conquest which turned Jerusalem into a Christian city. They were in Akko, Ashkelon, Tiberias and in other smaller settlements in the Galilee. Throughout the generations they were witness to the Persian invasion and to the Moslem conquerors who called Jerusalem "Al-Kuds", "The Holy". The Moslems built mosques; the crusaders converted these into churches and built fortresses in order to defend important crossroads. The first crusaders arrived in Israel from Europe in the 11th century with the declared intention of liberating the Church of the Holy Sepulchre in which, according to their belief, Jesus was buried after being taken down from the Cross. Their desire was to free the land from the Moslems and to establish the "Kingdom of Jerusalem," or "the Kingdom of David."

The territorial expansion of the ruling Crusaders reached its apex at the beginning of the 12th century, at which time it received a harsh blow from Salah-a-Din (Saladin) in the battle of Hittin (July of 1187). The last of the crusaders, the guardians of the kingdom, were expelled in the 13th century by the Mamelukes, Egyptian Moslems, and their final stronghold, Akko, fell in 1291. Palestine lost its international importance for several centuries. The remnants of the Jews survived primarily in the hills until the Turkish Ottoman conquest, which allowed the Jews to immigrate to Israel. At the end of the 16th century the Jews in Israel numbered approximately 50,000 and flourished for a brief time. However, in 1799, when Napoleon attempted unsuccessfully to conquer Israel, their number, once again, was small: approximately 5,000 of the area's 300,000 inhabitants.

Towards the end of the 19th century there began a revolutionary chapter in the history of the Jewish people and the land of Israel. The Zionist movement set out to fulfill the Zionist idea of establishing a Jewish state in the land of Israel.

In the settlements of the First Alia —so called because migration to Israel is not considered routine, but rather an ascent ("alia") to an exalted place— the foundations of modern agriculture were laid, as well as those of agricultural industry, such as wine production.

In 1909 the first kibbutz, Deganya, was founded at the spot where the Jordan River continues southward after separating from the Sea of Galilee (Kinneret), Israel's only fresh-water lake. The kibbutz was an interesting experiment in egalitarian, communal life based on personal labor, favoring joint education of the children, and, rather than being isolated entities, the kibbutzim encouraged their members to be involved in the life of the nation. In that same year, 1909, north of the Arab city of Jaffa, the foundations of the first Hebrew city, Tel Aviv, were laid, the city in white which is entirely a product of the 20th century.

The geopolitical location of the land of Israel at the junction of important commercial and strategic pathways of modern times was, since Napoleon's days, a cause of struggle on the part of superpowers for control in the region.

After the First World War, with the crumbling of the Ottoman Empire, the British Empire overcame the French and received a mandate over Israel. On the 29th of November 1947, the General Assembly of the United Nations decided upon a partitioning of the land into two states, a Palestinian state and a Jewish one, and upon an international Jerusalem.

On the 14th of May 1948, the first Prime Minister of the state of Israel, David Ben-Gurion, proclaimed the state's Declaration of Independence. The declaration promised a democratic, parliamentarian Israel, home and shelter to the refugees of the Holocaust in Europe and to all Jews of the Diaspora.

The War of Independence, which broke out the day after the United Nation's announcement of partition in 1947, was renewed more vigorously the day after the British withdrawal from Palestine on 15 May 1948, and was officially concluded in July of 1949. It shaped the borders of the state, which then changed only with the Six Day War in 1967. This war brought about the unification of Jerusalem, Israel's capital.

The first general population register of citizens of the state in November 1947 reflected a count of 782,000 citizens, of whom 713,000 were Jews. In its first four years of existence, the state absorbed almost 700,000 Jews, chiefly from the refugee camps of central and eastern Europe, the Balkan states, and from the Diaspora of Asia and Africa. These people learned to speak Hebrew, the official language of the state. The oldest among the immigrants from the east remember Arabic, the second official language of the state; however, their sons already absorb English words into the developing Hebrew slang.

Of the 5.3 million citizens of the state, about one million are minorities, most of whom are Arabs who live in villages, mainly in the Galilee, and in mixed cities such as Jaffa, Akko, Haifa, Ramla and Jerusalem. Most of them are Sunni Moslems. Others are Greek Catholics, Greek Orthodox, Roman Catholics and Maronites, Druze, Samaritans and followers of the Bahai faith.

The country's economic success is surely one of its greatest achievements: the country has few marketable natural resources, and suffers the burden of an enormous defense budget. Its one exportable commodity is brain power, with cutting-edge technology making several Israeli companies leaders in their fields.

Developers of many a designer fruit, flower or vegetable, Israelis' revolutionary approach to agriculture is world-famous. Using the Sea of Galilee as a national reservoir, water is pumped to the arid Negev, where such innovative solutions as drip irrigation are used to make the desert bloom. Meanwhile, nearly 200 million trees have been planted, restoring long-forgotten magnificence to barren hilltops.

There are few more obvious examples of Israel's diversity than its two major cities, Jerusalem and Tel Aviv. Although the distance between them is barely 60 kilometers, these two cities embody the dichotomy of Israel: Israel which shoulders its burden of history, its commitment to the Holy Land and to Jerusalem as the most holy; versus modern Israel which seeks universality, wishing to be as western as it can be, with Tel Aviv playing the role of a self-aware secular city.

The best way to see Jerusalem is by foot. With its seven open gates, ramparts and walkways easily accessible, the Old City walls beg for exploration. Enclosed within the 16th century limestone walls constructed by the Ottoman Sultan Suleiman the Magnificent, the Old City —unparalleled as a spiritual center to almost half the world's population— is endowed with dozens of sites rich in religious significance. While the Western Wall stands out as Judaism's holiest site, the Via Dolorosa and the Church of the Holy Sepulchre are sacred to Christians of all denominations, and the Al-Aksa Mosque and the magnificent Dome of the Rock stand at the fulcrum of Islam's third holiest city after Mecca and Medina.

In 1860 Jerusalem spread beyond the old walls and towards modern times and new prospects. Central to modern Jerusalem is the small area which contains Israel's parliament, the Knesset, scene of many a lively debate, as well as the new Supreme Court building and the government offices. Across the road stands the Hebrew University's Givat Ram campus, the Israel Museum and Shrine of the Book, permanent home to the world-famous Dead Sea Scrolls, the Science Museum and the Bible Lands Museum. Near the burial place of Theodore Herzl, founder of the World Zionist Organization, is Yad Vashem, Mount of Remembrance. It is a short walk from the memory of the Holocaust to the heritage of heroism and independence of Israel.

Memory and history play a major part in the fabric of Jerusalem, even in the daily life of the city.

In contrast, Tel Aviv (Hill of Spring) strives to ignore any commitment to history. Although it has a population numbering scarcely 350,000, compared with Jerusalem's 500,000, Tel Aviv lies at the center of a coastal plain metropolis encompassing some 2,000,000 inhabitants.

Not the prettiest of cities, Tel Aviv is considered to be a lively, though not a well preserved, museum of the Bauhaus style of the 1930s. Strolling along the seaside promenade, the beach appears as welcoming as a typical Mediterranean beach, the mosques and churches of Jaffa in the hazy south are as picturesque as one would expect an old and exotic town to be, and the luxury hotels nearby are as tempting and beckoning as any.

From its humble beginnings in 1909, when a group of Jewish immigrants bought a stretch of barren sand dunes north of the ancient port of Jaffa, Tel Aviv has developed into a modern metropolis. It is a trendy, fast-paced city "that never stops," a city that can rival most western capitals when it comes to night life, with pubs, cafes, clubs and discos staying open into the wee hours.

Adding to all these its lively commerce and numerous large financial institutions, Tel Aviv is geared to become the natural focus of a politically and economically healthy Middle East in times of "shalom," real peace.

Jerusalem and Tel Aviv are images in the eye of the photographer, who strives to capture fleeting moments of a reality in flux: sands, before they are transformed into homes for new immigrants; untouched seashores, before they evolve into buzzing tourist resorts; untamed cliffs in the wilderness, before they are turned into orderly nature reserves; and people, preserving traditional garb and customs 20 centuries old, before the 21st century bursts through their doors and into their homes. These images are the essence of this collection.

Page 15: Sunset accentuates the skyline of the old city of Akko, an ancient Canaanite port city at the northern edge of Haifa Bay. Today Akko is a Jewish-Arab city with a fishing port, Bahai center, churches, important mosques and crusader halls which host the Israel Fringe Theatre Festival in the autumn and the Vocal Music Festival in the spring.

Left: The interior of the large mosque built by Ahmed Al Jazzar, governor of Akko under the Ottoman Empire at the end of the 18th century. He built the mosque at the entrance to the city in 1781 upon the rubble of the Church of the Holy Cross. According to Islamic tradition, hairs from the prophet Mohammed's beard are preserved in the mosque and are exhibited to the public only on the 27th day of the month of Ramadan.

Top: The courtyard of the mosque of Ahmed Al Jazzar.

Above: Khan el-Umdan, in Arabic, "the inn of pillars". Built in 1785 during Al Jazzar's rule as an inn for travelers and merchants. The patio, circumscribed by an avenue of granite pillars brought from Caesarea, protected the guests, as well as their horses and livestock.

Above: Today this is a welcoming promenade. In the past, it was a wall which protected Akko from sea-borne enemies. Ahmed Al Jazzar built the wall, and in 1779 with the help of the British fleet, he foiled Napoleon's attack on the city using the cannons which were located on the wall.

Left: The marina and the fishing pier located in the crusader port in the southeastern part of the city.

Above: They arrived in this caravan site near Akko as a result of Operation Solomon in which 14,200 Jews from Ethiopia were brought to Israel in May 1991 during a 30-hour marathon. More than 1,000 people crowded into each jumbo jet, with planes landing and departing one after another, in one of the last heroic chapters of the Zionist myth.

Right: The children, at play, tease the camera with their glances and their movements, like true "sabras" from birth. The woman diverts her glance, finding it hard to look toward the camera.

19

Above: All the eye-soothing shades of green of Tel Dan. The Dan stream, which is one of the important sources of the Jordan River, flows here. Its path is lined by lush vegetation unusual in sunbaked Israel. Among the varied plant life found here is the Syrian Ash, growing to rare heights, as well as the fragrant laurel, better known as a spice.

Left: The homes of the first settlers in Metulla were refurbished, and the street retains the flavor of the founders' days. Metulla, an agricultural settlement in the upper Galilee, was founded in 1896 upon lands purchased with funds of the Baron de Rothschild from the Druze in the village of Umtulla, meaning "the observer". And indeed this is a pleasant resort village which overlooks the Golan Heights and the Lebanese Valley.

Above: The children are happy in the cold and very clear water of this pool in the Hurshat Tal ("Forest of Dew") nature reserve. Ancient oaks beautify the area, some of them hundreds of years old. Legend has it that followers of the prophet Mohammed stopped in the forest, and from the spears which they anchored into the ground in order to tie their horses, these great oaks sprouted.

Right: The shades of winter in the Hula Valley on the eastern edge of the upper Galilee. Farmers were concentrated around the lake in the valley's center for thousands of years. As a result of the Moslem wars against the crusaders, the valley was emptied of human life, the sources of the Jordan River overran the valley and turned it into swampland. Thus it remained until it was drained in 1951.

Page 24: The domes of the tomb of Rabbi Meir Baal Hanes ("the Miracle Maker") in Tiberias, located on the western shore of the Sea of Galilee. Some rabbis came to die in Tiberias. Others, however, preferred to seek healing in the famed therapeutic baths of the city, well known since the time of the Romans.

Above: On a clear day the skies are reflected a deep blue in the Sea of Galilee. The country's chief water reservoir is a mere 170 square kilometers. Located nearby are the remains of the oldest settlement in the region. Jesus preached in close proximity to the Sea of Galilee, fishermen draw their livelihood from it, poets addressed love songs to it, and today crowds of vacationers picnic in the shade of the palms along its beaches.

Left: In the inner courtyard of the tomb of Meir Baal Hanes, the miracle worker who lived in the 2nd century A.D. Believers in the healing and strengthening powers of the rabbi are offered holy water and portraits of holy men, alongside straw hats, to protect themselves from the intense sun of Tiberias.

Pages 22-23: Christian pilgrims pray and sing hymns at the Yardenit baptismal site at the spot of the Jordan River's separation from the Sea of Galilee. Greek Orthodox and Catholics reinstituted baptismal ceremonies at this peaceful place.

Above: The well preserved homes of the first settlers to Rosh Pinna attract people even today: city dwellers who have tired of urban life, Sixties refugees and members of experimental communes. The name of this settlement on the slopes of Mount Canaan means "cornerstone," and was given because in 1882 this was the first Jewish settlement in the Galilee in the new era.

Left: Green fields in the Hula Valley. Until the 1950s there were malaria-causing swamps here. The operation to drain the swamps lasted seven years and is considered an historic national effort. The fertile land which was uncovered is today used for agriculture, while a small reserve compensates Nature and its lovers for that which was sacrificed.

Above: Water flows again in the channels dug throughout the Hula Reserve in the northwest of the Hula lake which was drained. Man, who drained the area, helps Nature rebuild itself, showing an understanding of ecology which was not common in the past. In 1964 this became Israel's first nature reserve; today there are about 120 nature reserves.

Right: Pelicans return for a night's rest in the Hula Reserve at the end of April, on the way from Africa to their nesting sites in Europe.
In the autumn, about 75,000 of them will again choose this path which bisects Israel longitudinally and is popular among millions of migrating birds, much to the delight of the bird watchers.

Above: The Judas Tree with its purple-pink blossoms adorns a neighborhood in Safed, high in the shaded hills of the Galilee. Safed, a city sacred to Jews since the time of the Second Temple, became known in the 16th and 17th centuries as a center of Torah, mysticism and Kabbalah, and attracted Jews seeking redemption and preaching messianism.

Right: The ancient stone houses and iron sheds in the yards are covered with creeping vines in Peqiin in the Galilee. According to local tradition, there has been a Jewish presence in Peqiin since the time of the Second Temple. Today Druze, Christians, Moslems and Jews live in the community among their special houses of prayer, and a cave which is a site of pilgrimage for Jews.

Above: A boy's first haircut in a festivity near the grave of Rabbi Shimon Bar Yochai and his son Elazar, at the foot of Mount Meron (1,200 meters), in the Galilee. The festivity was first inaugurated in the 16th century by the mystics of Safed and it takes place every year on Lag B'Omer, the anniversary of the death of the rabbi. The throngs celebrate with singing and dancing, along with burning campfires and lit candles.

Above: Druze women enjoy a status different from that which is customary in the traditional Arab village society. Married women are exempt from the obligation to cover the face with veils, and in the case of divorce the woman is entitled to her share of the property. Like the rabbis' wives in Jewish religious society, the wives of the religious men assist their husbands in religious affairs.

Right: She is young and loves to dance. In her town, Deir al Asad in the Galilee, the young dance for fun in their free time, especially at engagement and wedding celebrations. Boys dance with boys, girls dance with girls, and the dances are accompanied by old folk songs, such as the traditional Moslem village chorus in which the girl sings: "I am not dancing because I am a foolish girl, but I dance for you, my groom, and for the daughters of your family."

Above: White turbans and dark clothes characterize the "wise men," the men of religion among the Druze, whose traditions are a close-guarded secret. Israeli Druze live in 18 villages in the Galilee and the Carmel. They separated from Islam in the 11th century and believe in God and seven prophets. It is difficult for a Druze to be accepted into this spiritual elite, which abstains from simple pleasures such as drinking, smoking, dancing and singing. These religious leaders shave their heads, but grow beards or mustaches of impressive size.

Above: Will he be a man of religion, a spiritual leader, or an officer in the Israel Defense Forces?

Top: The pyramid-shaped dome of the Basilica of the Annunciation dominates the urban landscape of the Galilean Nazareth. The Basilica was built between 1960 and 1969, above the crypt in which the Grotto of the Virgin Mary is located and on the ruins of a Byzantine church which was rebuilt by the crusaders.

Above: At prayer before the entrance to the Grotto, over which the Basilica of the Annunciation was built in Nazareth. It was here that the angel Gabriel informed the Virgin Mary that she would give birth to Jesus.

Right: Mount Tabor is prominent from every angle in the Jezreel Valley. Its geographic location made it the focus of battles from the days of Ramses II. At its summit, the miracle of the Transfiguration of Jesus took place before his disciples.

Right: A Franciscan monk strides alongside the remains of a Byzantine church. Upon these ruins and those of a crusader church the Basilica of the Transfiguration was built in 1923 on the summit of Mount Tabor. It was here that Jesus was transfigured before the eyes of his followers Peter, James and his brother John. "His face shone like the sun, and his garments became white as light" and Moses and Elijah appeared, speaking with him, as related in the first passages of Matthew 17.

Left: A carpet of chrysanthemums in the western Galilee. About 19% of all the wild flowers in Israel bear yellow flowers. From February through the late summer, one can enjoy the sight of the yellow fields as they attract a tremendous variety of pollen-gathering insects.

Top: The horse and its rider enjoy calm riding on the tracks of the Galilee as the late spring landscapes also play an active part in their pleasure. There is no professional horse racing in Israel, but riding for pleasure and galloping for show are quite common, and a number of ranches raise and cultivate elegant horses for sale.

Above: A bed of poppies against the natural oak groves of Mount Carmel. The poppy is the last of the wild red flowers to bloom each spring, while the anemone and the buttercup bloom earlier. Generally speaking, the red flowers are an unusual occurrence among the range of colors typical to the flora of the Mediterranean area. From April through June the poppies dominate the fields.

Above: The falls cross the natural pool in which the water temperature is a constant 28°c. In Arabic, this pool at the foot of Mount Gilboa in the Beit Shean Valley is called "Sachne" — in other words, hot. The residents of the Beit Shean Valley developed a garden around it in memory of three of their friends who were killed by a mine there in 1938. Its name is Gan Hashelosha.

Right: A moment of relaxation at the edge of the pool in Gan Hashelosha.

Above: Snappling above the Arch Cave in the western Galilee. Unless he is a completely righteous man, the climber should remain tied to his rope and not step on the arch, for it might collapse under him. This is the message behind a local Bedouin legend: Fearsome robbers decided to kill their repentant leader, but the good Lord caused the cave to collapse on them while he, who sat on the arch, was saved.

Left: A burial cave, one of tens of burial networks uncovered in the 1950s in Beit Shearim, on the border between the Jezreel Valley and the lower Galilee. Inside, sarcophagi were found, engraved with writings in Hebrew, Greek and Aramaic. The Jews fled here after the destruction of the Second Temple. It was here that the Sanhedrin, the supreme council of the jews, operated after the suppression of the Bar Kochba revolt of the 2nd century A.D.

Pages 38-39: The foot of the chalk hill appears to float upon the calm sea on a summer's day in Rosh Hanikra. From this point, the hill rises to a height of 70 meters. The top is a cliff overlooking the seashore in the upper Galilee, on the border between Israel and Lebanon, and the grotto is located under the surface of the water. The water currents carved 200 meter long grottos out of the soft chalk. Fauna and Flora unique to the area developed here, and nature lovers as well as the fishermen have learned to cherish it.

Above: The soft white chalk takes on a yellow-orange hue at sunset. Shadows of the visitors crossing the bridge opposite the entrance to the grottos bring movement and life to the bare stone.

Right: The light of day creeps hesitatingly into the grotto, bringing with it an air of mystery.

Above: The golden dome of the Bahai Shrine, which is the world center for this sect, is seen from everywhere in Haifa, which spreads expansively across the northern and western branches of the Carmel mountain range. From the mountain one can see the road crossing the German colony that was established at the end of the previous century by the Templars. The road leads to Israel's first modern port, which was opened in 1933 by the British in Israel's largest natural bay on the Mediterranean.

Left: The modest jetty established by the Phoenicians in the mid-3rd century B.C. in the northern Sharon area was transformed by Herod from 22 B.C. for twelve years into a major port and a maritime city called Caesarea, in honor of his Roman patron, Caesar Augustus. The crusaders later built a breakwater, deepening the water, and developed the port. Israeli archaeologists discovered a fascinating world here which had not yet been revealed entirely.

Left: The Roman theatre in the south of Caesarea, which dates from the second century, puts on its make-up and coloring and prepares for a performance of Verdi's opera, "Aida". During the summer the theatre is brimming with a range of musical and dance performances which draw thousands for each show. This is the oldest Roman theatre in Israel, and it is known for its superb acoustics. The western sea winds are the best possible amplifiers, as they pass across the stage from the back, carrying the notes towards the audience.

Above: Wedding photographers, too, find the antiquities of Caesarea to be a suitable backdrop for capturing the moments of happiness before the marriage. The yellow sunset softens the black-white contrast of the celebrants' clothes. The last joking of friends, farewell to bachelorhood. Soon the sun will set and the ceremony will begin. This moment will be preserved in the picture album.

Pages 44-45: Jerusalem. A panoramic view of the city from the summit of Mount Scopus.

Above: Water cools the dome of the Shrine of the Book, which was designed in the shape of the covers of the jars in which the Dead Sea scrolls were hidden. Opposite the shrine is the black basalt wall which symbolizes the children of darkness. The members of the Qumran sect considered themselves chosen by God, distinct from the rest of the world and from the people of Israel, whom they looked upon as children of darkness, and against whom their struggle would end in a war at the end of the world.

Left: A showcase in the form of a Torah scroll handle is prominent inside the Shrine of the Book in the Israel Museum in Jerusalem, Israel's largest museum. The Dead Sea Scrolls are preserved in the shrine, along with other findings from the Bar Kochba period. The scrolls, which were discovered in 1947 in Qumran near the Dead Sea, were written by members of the Judean Desert sect, which was identified with the Essenes, a Jewish sect that lived an ascetic life during the Second Temple period and was identified with the early Christians.

Above: Red hot chili pepper as a material, a color, a flavor and a smell: an object for joint creative art by children and their parents in a summer workshop in the Youth Wing of the Israel Museum. Art education in the museum began at the end of the 1950s in the attic of the Bezalel Treasure House even before the Israel Museum was established in 1965.

47

Above: The Church of the Visitation, also known as the Church of the Magnificat, stands out, especially bright among the dark cypress trees, in the clear air and picturesque village surroundings of Ein Karem, located in the southwest of Jerusalem. According to Christian tradition, the summer home of the parents of John the Baptist stood on this spot. It was here that Mary, mother of Jesus, while visiting her cousin Elizabeth, John's mother, first felt the movements of the baby in her womb.

Left: With the coming of the evening, the artificial light prevails even over the full moon, dramatically illuminating a section of the citadel wall, better known as the Tower of David. Housed within these walls, the Museum of the History of Jerusalem was opened in 1989, relating the story of the city through the use of the most advanced exhibition techniques.

Right: A pale morning light illuminates the cypress and olive trees surrounding the Church of St. Mary Magdalena, on the western slopes of the Mount of Olives. The Russian Czar Alexander III built this church — so Russian with its seven gold onion-shaped domes — in memory of his mother Maria Alexandrovna.

Left: The women gaze over the wall, watching the Procession of Palm Sunday, with the silver dome of the Church of the Holy Sepulchre, and the cross above it, behind them. Inside the church itself is the place from which "the three women", among them Mary Magdalena, watched the crucifixion of Jesus on the Golgotha hill, the name of which derives from its resemblance to a skull, "gulgolet" in Hebrew.

Left: Crowds of believers and tourists fill the courtyard at the entrance to the Church of the Holy Sepulchre in the Christian Quarter of the Old City. The last five stations of the Way of the Cross — and the burial place itself— are within the church. The church was built on the spot in which Helena, mother of the Byzantine emperor Constantinus, claimed to have found the cross resting upon the Golgotha stone.

Right: The Palm Sunday procession, which takes place on the last Sunday before Easter following the long period of fasting and penitance known as Lent, sets out from the church. Six Christian denominations jointly maintain the church and divide among themselves the times for mass and the processions. These groups are: Roman Catholics, Franciscans, Greek Orthodox, Armenians, Copts and Ethiopians.

Above: The architectural styles of the Church of
the Holy Sepulchre reveal its history: Upon the
ruins of a Roman temple, the emperor Constantinus
built the first church in the 4th century A.D.
Moslem zealots destroyed it in 1009. About 40
years later it was restored, and in 1099 the
crusaders added a new wing. In 1927 the church
was damaged by an earthquake. The carved stone
portals are the handiwork of Crusader craftsmen
from the 12th century.

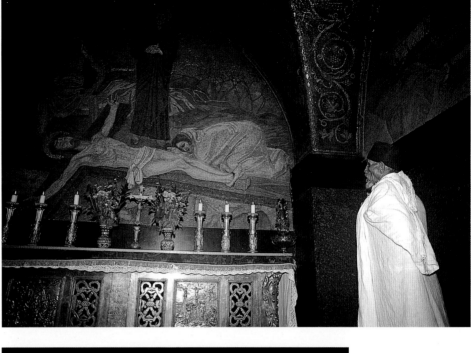

Top right: An Ethiopian cleric stands before the Altar of the Nails of the Holy Cross at Golgotha in the Church of the Holy Sepulchre. A group of Ethiopian monks resides on the roof of the church, and two chapels belong to them.

Right: In contemplation and prayer before candles lit by worshipers in the Church of the Holy Sepulchre.

Above: At the wedding, as on Sabbaths and holidays, the Belz Hassidim wear the silk caftans and fur hats ("shtreimel" in Yiddish), which originated in 18th century Poland, where this social-religious movement was founded. To them the rebbe is a saintly man who mediates between the Hassidim and their God, and frequently they sing and dance as a way of spiritually elevating the soul. The wine, poured from huge crystal decanters, certainly adds to the joy of the festivities.

Left: His father's socks, gleamingly white, confirm for this curious boy that he really is taking part in an important celebration. The Belz Hassidim are careful about their dress: on weekdays they wear fine black hats, white shirts and long black coats. Their pants, which are knee-length and tied in the back, are met by socks which are usually black, but are replaced by white on holidays.

Left: Never in his life has he seen a celebration like this: 5,000 square meters of tent space for the guests, 600,000 liters of soft drinks, 20,000 eggs, 7.5 tons of potatoes, 40,000 celebrants at the wedding of the son of the Belzer Rebbe in Jerusalem. And this is only the third time in his life that the groom (18 years old) has ever seen his bride (also 18).

Above: Facing the Holy Ark, which stands on the eastern wall towards the direction of the Temple, in a synagogue in Mea Shearim.

Left: Placed according to tradition in the window, these fully lit Chanuka lamps indicate that it is the last night of the holiday in Mea Shearim, Jerusalem's ultra-orthodox neighborhood which was founded in 1875. One of the first neighborhoods built outside the Old City walls, Mea Shearim is nonetheless surrounded by its own intangible walls against modernity and the Zionist state.

Above: Ultra-orthodox girls behind the window bars: between the world inside and the world outside. Women here are taught to support and be of assistance to the husband, who studies Torah. They are expected not to take part in public life. In response, the women have developed their own special social life and leisure activities.

Right: An ultra-orthodox woman concentrates firmly while looking at kerchiefs. She is well dressed from head to foot, but she will not give up having an aesthetic head covering, matching the colors of her dress. Fashions in clothing and head coverings, from kerchiefs and hair-nets to wigs, surpass even the rabbis' orders, which call for modesty and simplicity of dress in women.

Left: Wrapped in the flag of the state of Israel as in a tallith (prayer shawl) and wearing a matching hat, he sits in the plaza before the Western Wall, known in Hebrew as the "kotel". Is this his declaration of the complex tie between nation and religion in Judaism, or is he a manifestation of "the Jerusalem syndrome", an outbreak of madness in some visitors to this charged city? Since the 13th century, the Kotel has been holy to the Jews as a national and religious symbol. The remaining western portion of the wall which surrounded the Temple Mount in the days of the Second Temple, the Kotel is revered because it is believed to have been the closest to the Holy of Holies where the Holy Ark stood.

Above: Deep in prayer this worshiping Jew stands in front of the Kotel, a book of Psalms in his hands, but knowing the prayers by heart. In the spaces between the lower stones of the Herodian period — which were put in place without mortar— people insert notes of entreaty and prayer. It is, in its way, a personal bond between the supplicant and the Divine Spirit, which never left the Kotel from the time of the destruction of the Second Temple in 70 A.D. The tears which accompany this ritual have lent the Kotel its other name, "the Wailing Wall".

Right: On Fridays, throngs of Moslem worshipers crowd into the area between the Dome of the Rock and the Al-Aksa mosque for public prayer. Their numbers often reach 70,000 with people coming from Jerusalem as well as other areas of the country. According to Islamic custom, they face towards the Saudi Arabian city of Mecca, the birthplace of Mohammed, the last of the prophets of Allah.

Below: Only males worship in public. The women are not active in prayer, and they observe the worshipers from afar, in a space provided for them. The Imam commences and the prayers begin. The men, standing erect in rows, bow to the ground behind the row in front of them, and murmur the words of prayer. When they finish, all rise as one man.

Above: The Dome of the Rock was built as a shrine, not as a mosque, by Caliph Abd al-Malik ibn Marwan of the Ummayad dynasty in the year 691, and not by the Caliph Omar, as some believe mistakenly. It was built in order to protect the rock on the Temple Mount from which, according to Moslem tradition, Mohammed ascended to heaven on the back of his horse Al-Burak after meeting with the prophets who preceded him near the Holy of Holies of the Jewish people. This perfect building is an octagon within an octagon containing a round structure which hides the rock. Above is a drum which supports the gold-plated bronze dome.

Above: The wondrous appearance of the Dome of the Rock is magnified by the blue and gold ceramic tiles which cover the outer walls. The ceramic tiles replaced the original mosaic which was damaged by the sun and the passage of time. Sinan, architect of the Ottoman sultan Suleiman the Magnificent, redesigned the external decorations and ordered the tiles from Turkey. The lower portion of the wall is covered in marble panels which are recognizable as Byzantine art. The marble panels were placed side by side in such a manner as to form symmetric patterns to perfection.

A shop in the market ("souk") in the Old City in
East Jerusalem. A selection of seeds, nuts, dried
figs, dates and spices produced in Israel and
imported from abroad produce aromas no less
exotic than the appearance of the place itself.
Markets developed around the Church of the Holy
Sepulchre in crusader Jerusalem, which were filled
by pilgrims who sought money changers,
inexpensive restaurants and clothing and bought
souvenirs and local handicrafts. All this can be
found in the souk today as well.

The watermelons are a deeper shade of red in the Makhane Yehuda market, thanks to the artificial lighting of the roofed marketplace in the center of the city. The latest hit in the summer is seedless watermelon, a development of science. More than it is an attraction to tourists and those in search of exotic Oriental products, it is meant for local buyers who come to the market to purchase fresh, inexpensive food products.

Above: In 1860, Jerusalem expanded beyond its
ancient walls and its neighborhoods spread out
upon the surrounding hills. Each neighborhood has
its own character created by the people who chose
to live in it, and its unique color, created by the
combinations of the age of the stone houses, the
appearance of the roof and the illumination of the
sun at each and every hour of the day.

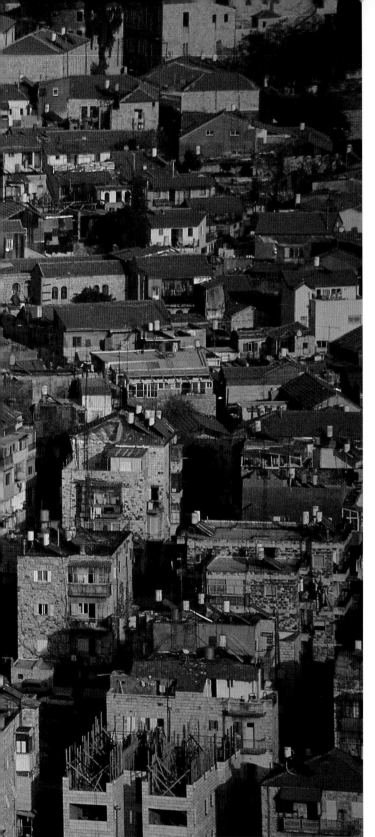

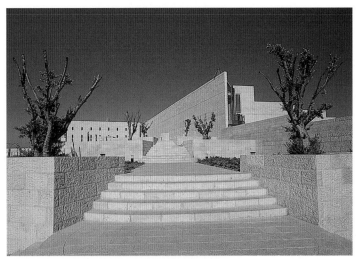

Top: The stones of the new Supreme Court building in Jerusalem are new and still white. In October 1992 the building was inaugurated, located close to the parliament of Israel, the Knesset. The combinations of straight lines, symbolizing law, and curved lines, a metaphor for justice, characterize this building, which quotes extensively —and consciously— symbolic sites around Jerusalem, such as the Kotel.

Above: The building of the Y.M.C.A. (Young Men's Christian Association), inaugurated in 1933 in the center of Jerusalem, have already darkened. It expresses the style of architects from the British school, who tried during the period of the British Mandate to create a "Land of Israel" style through the eclectic use of local Arabic architectural elements, Jerusalem stone, and Christian motifs. The tower holds the Middle East's only carillon of bells, and in the summertime one may hear their chiming in bell concerts.

Top: From Jaffa on the hill, one can see its former northern suburb, Ahuzat Bayit, founded in 1909, today completely different from the vision of its founders, who pictured it as a quiet city of gardens. That suburb became a city, lively Tel Aviv (Hill of Spring), a commercial, financial and cultural center in Israel, reunited with Jaffa under one joint municipality since 1949.

Above: A renovated building in white in the pedestrian mall of Nahalat Binyamin. Originally this was a neighborhood with an East European character, established by Jewish craftsmen from Jaffa in the 1920s. Today the street is lined with stands put there by artists, and sellers of odd items, as well as by cafes which put tables outside under awnings in the street.

Above: The seafront in Jaffa at the base of the reconstructed part from the time of the Turks. Jaffa, an ancient port city dating from the time of the Canaanites at the end of the fourth millenia B.C., although its name has been tied to that of Japhet, son of Noah. The port of Haifa replaced the port of Jaffa, which was closed in 1965. Today it is a fishing port and a pier for small boats and yachts. The ancient city, once restored, became a center for art and entertainment.

Above: The courtyard of the girls' school in the Neve Zedek neighborhood, which was renovated and turned into the Israeli Dance Center. Neve Zedek was founded in 1887 as the first attempt to establish a Jewish neighborhood on the outskirts of Jaffa. Its special atmosphere attracted poets and writers at the beginning and today it attracts designers and architects who renovate the neighborhood's distinctive buildings and reconstruct the spirit of Little Tel Aviv.

Right: The IBM building, America House, and between them Europe House form an elegant center in Tel Aviv. A city which lacks its own style and loves to adopt the latest international building styles.

Above: Crowds of Israelis have gathered along the shore of Tel Aviv to watch the demonstration conducted by the air force and the navy of the IDF (Israel Defence Forces) on Independence Day.

Left: The grass at Tel Aviv University is always green. The university was at first a branch of the Hebrew University of Jerusalem, late in the 1950s. Since its founding in 1965, the university has become a large campus with modern buildings and spectacular landscaping. To the left, the central library building; in front, the Nahum Goldman Museum of the Jewish Diaspora (Beit Hatefutsoth).

Above: Nature and culture are joined in the spring festival at the bell cave in Beit Guvrin. Along with the audience, the musicians, veteran Israelis as well as new immigrants, enjoy the superb acoustics of the cave. Thousands of caves like this one have been found in the coastal plain between the sea and the Judean hills. These chalk white and beige limestone caves were carved out, for the most part, from the 7th to the 10th centuries in order to extract raw materials for building.

Right: The natural pagodas of the Soreq cave in the Avshalom Nature Reserve in the Judean hills cannot bear light, loud noises and crowds. Only the sound of dripping water is heard in the cave which Nature hid from the eyes of man for millions of years, until its chance discovery in 1968. The contact between water droplets and limestone and the gas formed upon contact create the stalactites which drip from the ceiling and meet the stalagmites which rise from the floor of the cave.

Above: An old tractor, bunches of hay, flowers and rejoicing children in the celebrations of the Feast of Weeks (Shavuot),at Kibbutz Ein Shemer. This agricultural spring holiday in honor of the first harvest is also a traditional Jewish holiday which notes the time of the giving of the Torah on Mount Sinai. The holiday gives the kibbutz a chance to show the audience —mostly city dwellers— a kibbutz tradition which has become a staged performance.

Right: The greenhouses of the cooperative village Ein Yahav in the Arava, neutralize the seasons of the year: controlled temperatures and sophisticated watering using computerized drip irrigation enable the farmers to offer melons, eggplants, peppers and tomatoes even out of season.

Above: The road winding down from the Judean hills to the lowest place on earth, 398 meters below sea level, the Dead Sea. It is because of the saltiness of the water that no life exists in the sea; thus, its name in Hebrew, the Salt Sea.

Page 72: Masada (the Hebrew word for "fortress") is seen here from the air, isolated at the top of a cliff as if guarding still its secret. The great story of Masada is the story of the suicide of 967 zealots, led by Elazar Ben-Yair. They preferred death rather than facing surrender to the Romans after the destruction of the Second Temple. Their story was adopted by the Israeli society as a myth of heroism and sacrifice for the sake of national sovereignty.

Above: A huge, sphinx-shaped shadow is cast towards the Great Rift Valley, which includes the Dead Sea.

Above: The wealth of minerals to be found in the Dead Sea can be identified in the color of the water. The Dead Sea is about 50 kilometers long, and some of it is used as health spas. The water has therapeutic qualities and along its shores are sulfur springs, some of which are warm, and all of which are healthful.

Left: On a dried inlet of the sea one feels as if on a deserted island. The layers of air above this low place act as an efficient filter to the ultra-violet sun rays, and the damage done by sunbathing here is reduced. Still, it's best not to pass up the sun umbrella here, either.

Top: The colors of a dried mineral-rich sea. The lower portion of the Dead Sea is drying up both because of overuse of the waters of the Jordan River, which is the main source of the Dead Sea, and because of the small quantities of rain in the area.

Above: The potassium looks like snow, in a place which has never seen snow. A salt coast at the potassium factories in Sedom. The salt pans have been a familiar part of the Dead Sea area's landscape since the 1930s. Recently there has been a growing awareness of the conflict between the preservation of nature and ancient landscapes and the need to exploit natural resources for the benefit of industry and the economy.

Above: Mount Sedom as a relief. Running along the western shore of the Dead Sea, this mountain ascends to a height of 230 meters above the level of the Dea Sea. The chalk and lime carbonate of which the pale clay earth of Mount Sedom is composed are the cause of the colors found in the area.

Left: The Perazim wadi, as its Hebrew name implies, is wild and jumps in all directions. It is a dry stream to the south of the Dead Sea. The flood waters which cut deep grooves have disappeared, leaving only the grooves spreading out in all directions.

Above: Without any serious competitors, the Ibex, a protected mountain goat, is the most photographed animal in the Ein Gedi region.

Above: A wheat field after harvest in the northern Negev, the granary of the state of Israel.

Left: Bedouin women, in private conversation, in the northern Negev. Since 1948, these people of the desert —Badiya, in Arabic— have changed from nomadic tribes, mostly goat herders, to settlers in small towns and permanent settlements which were organized for them in a process which was met by objection, but which obligated them to find new occupations and to reconcile themselves to the penetration of modernity into their society.

Above: Thousands of archaeological excavations take place in Israel, such as Avdat in the central Negev mountain. Avdat's name was given by its founders, the Nabateans, in the 4th century B.C., in honor of their king, Oboda the Second. The Nabatean station along the spice route was conquered by the Romans, flourished as a city during the Byzantine period, and waned following the Moslem conquest in the 7th century A.D., until it was completely abandoned in the 10th century.

Right: The Ein Avdat National Park, a canyon in the Negev north of the city of Avdat. Spring water flows in natural pools to the deep crack of the Zin wadi. Flood waters, which cannot be absorbed by the hardened, desiccated earth, rush in foaming currents that snatch up everything in their path and carve out shapes on the canyon walls. Water remaining in pools reflects the color of the clear, cloudless skies.

Above: The southern gateway to the state of Israel is painted the deep shade of blue which is particular to the cool waters of the Gulf of Eilat. From here one can see the peaceful shore of the most important resort town in Israel. Its strategic location on the commercial route between East and West brought many conquerors to the city. From the year of its founding as a city in Israel (1951), Eilat has developed as a tourist spot free of historical burdens, wishing no more than to please its visitors, who find there an ever-shining sun, freedom, vacation activities and water sports.

Left: Tourists are not the only ones who come to vacation in Eilat; Israelis, too, come to relax and forget their daily troubles, to "recharge their batteries" and "catch some sun" without worrying about UV and other existential hazards.

And finally, a group picture. Their backs to the view
and their faces smiling for the trusty photo album,
guardian of memories from the journey. But there's
more to come, because it's good to gather the
memories into an album, but it's even better to
keep traveling and collecting them.

*

All rights reserved. No part of this book may be
reproduced, stored in a retrieval system, or
transmitted in any form or by any means,
electronic, mechanical, photocopying, recording or
otherwise, without prior written permission of the
publisher.